Signs Are Everywhere

by Myka-Lynne Sokoloff

 HOUGHTON MIFFLIN HARCOURT
School Publishers

PHOTOGRAPHY CREDITS: **Cover** (bkgd) Rubens Abboud/Alamy, (inset) steven langerman/Alamy. **1** Mikael Karlsson/Alamy. **2** (l) Rubens Abboud/Alamy, (r) Steven Langerman/Alamy. **3** (b) Donald Miralle/Getty Images, (t) AA World Travel Library/Alamy. **4** (l) Stock Images/Alamy, (r) Barry Mason/Alamy. **5** © Dennis MacDonald/age fotostock **6** Mikael Karlsson/Alamy. **7** (r) Comstock/Jupiter Images, (l) © Jean-Pierre Lescourret/CORBIS. **8** © Ramin Talaie/CORBIS. **9** Carsten Reisinger/Alamy.

Printed in China

ISBN-13: 978-0-547-02953-5
ISBN-10: 0-547-02953-5

13 14 15 16 0940 19 18 17 16
4500569761

Look around your school and
around your town.
What signs do you see?
Signs are everywhere.
They hang on posts, on walls,
and on doors.
They help you in many ways.

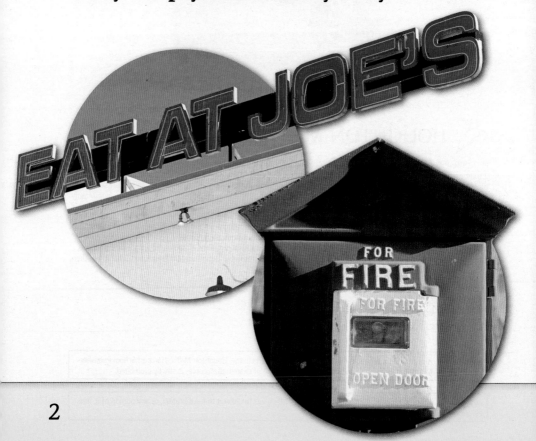

Signs can tell you what to do.
They can tell you to be polite.
Signs can also tell you to cheer
for your team.

Signs can also tell you what
not to do.
They can tell you to keep off
the grass.
They can also tell you not to dive.
Signs like this help keep you safe.

At school, this trash needs to be cleared away.
The teacher's assistant put up some signs.
One tells where the plastic should go.
Another tells where the paper should go.

Stop signs tell cars to stop.
This truck failed to stop
and crashed.
Is the driver in trouble now?
Yes, he should have read the sign!

Some signs use numbers.
The numbers on your house tell
where you live.
The numbers on your library books
tell where the books are kept in
the library.

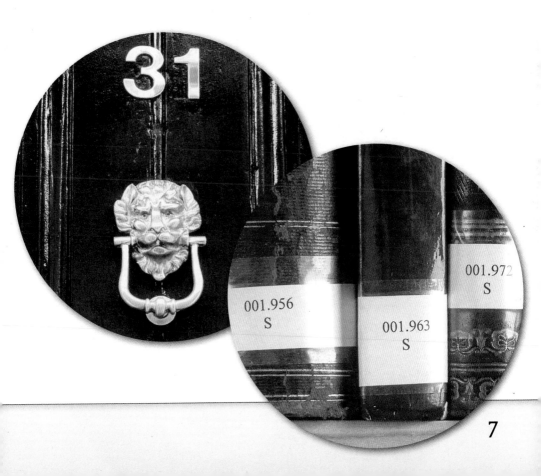

Some signs have no words
or numbers.
They use pictures instead.
People agreed on what these
pictures mean so everyone can
understand them.
Some signs use pictures to help
drivers know where to go.

What would happen if people started tearing down signs? People might forget to follow the rules. People might forget to be safe. What a mess that would be!

Pay attention to the signs you see.
Sometimes the signs have a lot
of wisdom.
They can help you in many ways!

Responding

Word Builder

What are some ways that you can be polite to adults or other children? Copy the web and fill in the rest of the circles.

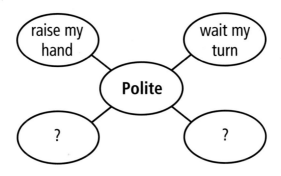

Write About It

Text to Self Think about a sign that tells you to be polite. Then write a few sentences that tell what the sign says, where it is, and why it helps you to be polite.

✔ **TARGET STRATEGY** **Question** Ask questions about what you are reading.

Word Teaser What do you get from working hard at school?